THE COMMON CORE

Clarifying Expectations for Teachers & Students

ENGLISH LANGUAGE ARTS

Grade 5

Created and Presented by
Align, Assess, Achieve

Mc Graw Hill Education

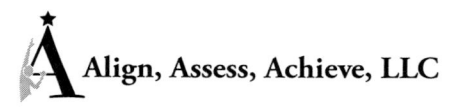 **Align, Assess, Achieve, LLC**

STEM McGraw-Hill is committed to providing instructional materials in Science,
Technology, Engineering, and Mathematics (STEM) that give all students a solid
foundation, one that prepares them for college and careers in the 21st century.

Send all inquiries to:
McGraw-Hill Education
STEM Learning Solutions Center
8787 Orion Place
Columbus, OH 43240

ISBN: 978-002-123293-2
MHID: 0-02-123293-8

Printed in the United States of America.

5 6 7 8 9 GLO 16 15 14 13

STEM

Our mission is to provide educational resources
that enable students to become the problem solvers
of the 21st century and inspire them to explore
careers within Science, Technology, Engineering,
and Mathematics (STEM) related fields.

Acknowledgements

This book integrates the Common Core State Standards – a framework for educating students to be competitive at an international level – with well-researched instructional planning strategies for achieving the goals of the CCSS. Our work is rooted in the thinking of brilliant educators, such as Grant Wiggins, Jay McTighe, and Rick Stiggins, and enriched by our work with a great number of inspiring teachers, administrators, and parents. We hope this book provides a meaningful contribution to the ongoing conversation around educating lifelong, passionate learners.

We would like to thank many talented contributors who helped create *The Common Core: Clarifying Expectations for Teachers and Students*. Our authors, Lani Meyers and Mindy Holmes, for their intelligence, persistence, and love of teaching; Graphic Designer Thomas Davis, for his creative talents and good nature through many trials; Editors, Laura Gage and Dr. Teresa Dempsey, for their educational insights and encouragement; Director of book editing and production Josh Steskal, for his feedback, organization, and unwavering patience; Our spouses, Andrew Bainbridge and Tawnya Holman, who believe in our mission and have, through their unconditional support and love, encouraged us to take risks and grow.

Katy Bainbridge
Bob Holman
Co-Founders
Align, Assess, Achieve, LLC

Executive Editors: *Katy Bainbridge and Bob Holman*
Authors: *Mindy Holmes and Lani Meyers*
Contributing Authors: *Teresa Dempsey, Katy Bainbridge and Bob Holman*
Graphic Design & Layout: *Thomas Davis; thomasanceldesign.com*
Director of Book Editing & Production: *Josh Steskal*

Introduction

Purpose

The Common Core State Standards (CCSS) provide educators across the nation with a shared vision for student achievement. They also provide a shared challenge: how to interpret the standards and use them in a meaningful way? Clarifying the Common Core was designed to facilitate the transition to the CCSS at the district, building, and classroom level.

Organization

Clarifying the Common Core presents content from two sources: the CCSS and Align, Assess, Achieve. Content from the CCSS is located in the top section of each page and includes the strand, CCR, and grade level standard. The second section of each page contains content created by Align, Assess, Achieve – Enduring Understandings, Essential Questions, Suggested Learning Targets, and Vocabulary. The black bar at the bottom of the page contains the CCSS standard identifier. A sample page can be found in the next section.

Planning for Instruction and Assessment

This book was created to foster meaningful instruction of the CCSS. This requires planning both quality instruction and assessment. Designing and using quality assessments is key to high-quality instruction (Stiggins et al.). Assessment should accurately measure the intended learning and should inform further instruction. This is only possible when teachers and students have a clear vision of the intended learning. When planning instruction it helps to ask two questions, "Where am I taking my students?" and "How will we get there?" The first question refers to the big picture and is addressed with **Enduring Understandings** and **Essential Questions**. The second question points to the instructional process and is addressed by **Learning Targets**.

Where Am I Taking My Students?

When planning, it is useful to think about the larger, lasting instructional concepts as **Enduring Understandings**. Enduring Understandings are rooted in multiple units of instruction throughout the year and are often utilized K-12. These concepts represent the lasting understandings that transcend your content. Enduring Understandings serve as the ultimate goal of a teacher's instructional planning. Although tempting to share with students initially, we do not recommend telling students the Enduring Understanding in advance. Rather, Enduring Understandings are developed through meaningful engagement with an Essential Question.

(continued on next page)

Essential Questions work in concert with Enduring Understandings to ignite student curiosity. These questions help students delve deeper and make connections between the concepts and the content they are learning. Essential Questions are designed with the student in mind and do not have an easy answer; rather, they are used to spark inquiry into the deeper meanings (Wiggins and McTighe). Therefore, we advocate frequent use of Essential Questions with students. It is sometimes helpful to think of the Enduring Understanding as the answer to the Essential Question.

How Will We Get There?

If Enduring Understandings and Essential Questions represent the larger, conceptual ideas, then what guides the learning of specific knowledge, reasoning, and skills? These are achieved by using **Learning Targets**. Learning Targets represent a logical, student friendly progression of teaching and learning. Targets are the scaffolding students climb as they progress towards deeper meaning.

There are four types of learning targets, based on what students are asked to do: knowledge, reasoning/understanding, skill, and product (Stiggins et al.). When selecting Learning Targets, teachers need to ask, "What is the goal of instruction?" After answering this question, select the target or targets that align to the instructional goal.

Instructional Goal	Target Type	Key Verbs
Recall basic information and facts	Knowledge (K)	Name, identify, describe
Think and develop an understanding	Reasoning/ Understanding (R)	Explain, compare and contrast, predict
Apply knowledge and reasoning	Skill (S)	Use, solve, calculate
Synthesize to create original work	Product (P)	Create, write, present

Adapted from Stiggins et al. *Classroom Assessment for Student Learning.* (Portland: ETS, 2006). Print.

Keep in mind that the Enduring Understandings, Essential Questions, and Learning Targets in this book are suggestions. Modify and combine the content as necessary to meet your instructional needs. Quality instruction consists of clear expectations, ongoing assessment, and effective feedback. Taken together, these promote meaningful instruction that facilitates student mastery of the Common Core State Standards.

References

Stiggins, Rick, Jan Chappuis, Judy Arter, and Steve Chappuis. *Classroom Assessment for Student Learning.* 2nd. Portland, OR: ETS, 2006.

Wiggins, Grant, and Jay McTighe. *Understanding by Design, Expanded 2nd Edition.* 2nd. Alexandria, VA: ASCD, 2005.

Page Organization

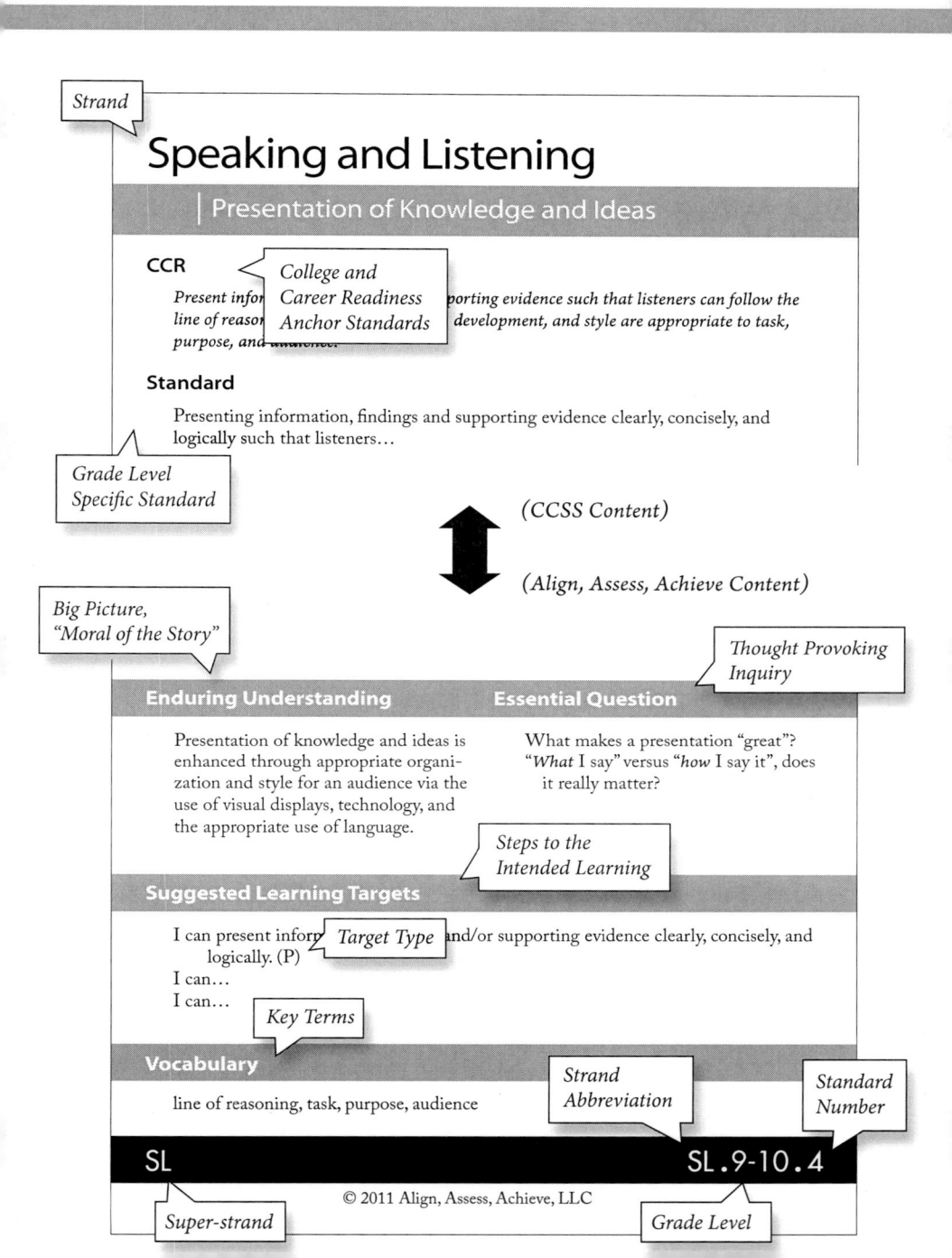

Strand

Speaking and Listening

Presentation of Knowledge and Ideas

CCR — *College and Career Readiness Anchor Standards*

Present infor... ...porting evidence such that listeners can follow the line of reaso... ...development, and style are appropriate to task, purpose, and ...

Standard

Presenting information, findings and supporting evidence clearly, concisely, and logically such that listeners…

Grade Level Specific Standard

(CCSS Content)

(Align, Assess, Achieve Content)

Big Picture, "Moral of the Story"

Thought Provoking Inquiry

Enduring Understanding

Presentation of knowledge and ideas is enhanced through appropriate organization and style for an audience via the use of visual displays, technology, and the appropriate use of language.

Essential Question

What makes a presentation "great"? "*What* I say" versus "*how* I say it", does it really matter?

Steps to the Intended Learning

Suggested Learning Targets

I can present infor... *Target Type* ...and/or supporting evidence clearly, concisely, and logically. (P)
I can…
I can…

Key Terms

Vocabulary

line of reasoning, task, purpose, audience

Strand Abbreviation

Standard Number

SL

SL.9-10.4

Super-strand

Grade Level

© 2011 Align, Assess, Achieve, LLC

Literature

CCR

Read closely to determine what the text says explicitly and to make logical inferences from it; cite specific textual evidence when writing or speaking to support conclusions drawn from the text.

Standard

Quote accurately from a text when explaining what the text says explicitly and when drawing inferences from the text.

Enduring Understanding

Effective readers use a variety of strategies to make sense of key ideas and details presented in text.

Essential Questions

What do good readers do?
Am I clear about what I just read?
How do I know?

Suggested Learning Targets

I can quote ("word for word" support) accurately from a text. (S)
I can define inference and explain how a reader uses direct quotes from a text to reach a logical conclusion ("based on what I've read, it's most likely true that…"). (R)
I can read closely and find answers explicitly in text (right there answers) and answers that require an inference. (S)
I can analyze an author's words and find quotes needed to support both explicit and inferential questions. (S)

Vocabulary

quote, inference, explicit

R   RL.5.1

Literature

CCR

Determine central ideas or themes of a text and analyze their development; summarize the key supporting details and ideas.

Standard

Determine a theme of a story, drama, or poem from details in the text, including how characters in a story or drama respond to challenges or how the speaker in a poem reflects upon a topic; summarize the text.

Enduring Understanding

Effective readers use a variety of strategies to make sense of key ideas and details presented in text.

Essential Questions

What do good readers do?
Am I clear about what I just read?
How do I know?

Suggested Learning Targets

I can define theme (a lesson the author is revealing – *Honesty is the best policy.*). (K)
I can analyze details in a text (e.g. how characters respond to challenges or how the speaker in a poem reflects upon a topic) to determine a theme (author's overall message). (R)
I can define summary (a shortened version of the text that states the key points). (K)
I can compose a summary stating the key points of the text. (P)

Vocabulary

theme, summary

R

RL.5.2

Literature

CCR

Analyze how and why individuals, events, and ideas develop and interact over the course of a text.

Standard

Compare and contrast two or more characters, settings, or events in a story or drama, drawing on specific details in the text (e.g., how characters interact).

Enduring Understanding

Effective readers use a variety of strategies to make sense of key ideas and details presented in text.

Essential Questions

What do good readers do?
Am I clear about what I just read?
How do I know?

Suggested Learning Targets

I can identify characters, settings, and events in a story or drama. (K)
I can compare (determine similarities) two or more characters, settings, or events in a story or drama using specific details from the text. (R)
I can contrast (determine differences) two or more characters, settings, or events in a story or drama using specific details from the text. (R)

Vocabulary

compare, contrast

R

RL.5.3

Literature

CCR

Interpret words and phrases as they are used in a text, including determining technical, connotative, and figurative meanings, and analyze how specific word choices shape meaning or tone.

Standard

Determine the meaning of words and phrases as they are used in a text, including figurative language such as metaphors and similes.

Enduring Understanding

Analyzing texts for structure, purpose, and viewpoint allows an effective reader to gain insight and strengthen understanding.

Essential Questions

Author's choice: Why does it matter? What makes a story a "great" story?

Suggested Learning Targets

I can use various strategies (e.g., context clues, root words, affixes) to determine the meaning of words and phrases. (S)
I can define and identify various forms of figurative language (e.g., simile, metaphor, personification, alliteration, onomatopoeia). (K)
I can distinguish between literal language (it means exactly what it says) and figurative language (sometimes what you say is not exactly what you mean). (R)

Vocabulary

figurative language, literal language

R

RL.5.4

Literature

CCR

Analyze the structure of texts, including how specific sentences, paragraphs, and larger portions of the text (e.g., a section, chapter, scene, or stanza) relate to each other and the whole.

Standard

Explain how a series of chapters, scenes, or stanzas fits together to provide the overall structure of a particular story, drama, or poem.

Enduring Understanding

Analyzing texts for structure, purpose, and viewpoint allows an effective reader to gain insight and strengthen understanding.

Essential Questions

Author's choice: Why does it matter?
What makes a story a "great" story?

Suggested Learning Targets

I can recognize that chapters are found in stories, scenes are found in dramas, and stanzas are found in poems. (K)
I can explain how chapters, scenes, and stanza fit together to form stories, dramas, or poems. (R)

Vocabulary

chapter, scene, stanza

R   RL.5.5

Literature

Craft and Structure

CCR

Assess how point of view or purpose shapes the content and style of a text.

Standard

Describe how a narrator's or speaker's point of view influences how events are described.

Enduring Understanding

Analyzing texts for structure, purpose, and viewpoint allows an effective reader to gain insight and strengthen understanding.

Essential Questions

Author's choice: Why does it matter? What makes a story a "great" story?

Suggested Learning Targets

I can identify basic points of view as first person (narrator tells about her/himself; "I"), second person (narrator talks directly to reader; "you"), or third person (narrator tells about others; "he/she/it"). (K)
I can determine a narrator's or speaker's point of view in a text. (R)
I can describe how events in a text are influenced by point of view. (S)

Vocabulary

point of view, first person, second person, third person, influence

R

RL.5.6

Literature

CCR

*Integrate and evaluate content presented in diverse media and formats, including visually and quantitatively, as well as in words.**

Standard

Analyze how visual and multimedia elements contribute to the meaning, tone, or beauty of a text (e.g., graphic novel, multimedia presentation of fiction, folktale, myth, poem).

Please see "Research to Build and Present Knowledge" in Writing and "Comprehension and Collaboration" in Speaking and Listening for additional standards relevant to gathering, assessing, and applying information from print and digital sources.

Enduring Understanding

To gain keener insight into the integration of knowledge and ideas, effective readers analyze and evaluate content, reasoning, and claims in diverse formats.

Essential Questions

In what ways does creative choice impact an audience?
Whose story is it, and why does it matter?

Suggested Learning Targets

I can identify visual elements found in a text (e.g., photographs, drawings, cartoons). (K)
I can analyze how visual elements add meaning, create tone, and contribute to the beauty of a text. (R)
I can analyze multimedia presentations of a text and determine how a media presentation adds to the meaning, tone, and beauty of an original text. (R)

Vocabulary

visual element, multimedia, tone

R   RL.5.7

Literature

CCR

Delineate and evaluate the argument and specific claims in a text, including the validity of the reasoning as well as the relevance and sufficiency of the evidence.

Standard

(Not applicable to literature)

(No Common Core State Standard #8 for Reading and Literature)

R

RL.5.8

Literature

CCR

Analyze how two or more texts address similar themes or topics in order to build knowledge or to compare the approaches the authors take.

Standard

Compare and contrast stories in the same genre (e.g., mysteries and adventure stories) on their approaches to similar themes and topics.

Enduring Understanding

To gain keener insight into the integration of knowledge and ideas, effective readers analyze and evaluate content, reasoning, and claims in diverse formats.

Essential Questions

In what ways does creative choice impact an audience?

Whose story is it, and why does it matter?

Suggested Learning Targets

I can define theme (a lesson the author is revealing – *Honesty is the best policy.*). (K)

I can identify similar themes and topics found in stories from the same genre. (K)

I can compare (determine similarities) how stories in the same genre can communicate the same theme or topic. (R)

I can contrast (determine differences) how stories in the same genre can communicate the same theme or topic. (R)

Vocabulary

compare, contrast, theme, genre

R   RL.5.9

Literature

CCR

Read and comprehend complex literary and informational texts independently and proficiently.

Standard

By the end of the year, read and comprehend literature, including stories, dramas, and poetry, at the high end of the grades 4–5 text complexity band independently and proficiently.

Enduring Understanding

Students who are college and career ready read and interpret a variety of complex texts with confidence and independence.

Essential Questions

What do good readers do?
Am I clear about what I just read?
How do I know?

Suggested Learning Targets

I can closely read complex grade level texts. (S)
I can reread a text to find more information or clarify ideas. (S)
I can use reading strategies (e.g., ask questions, make connections, take notes, make inferences, visualize, re-read) to help me understand difficult complex text. (S)

Vocabulary

reading strategy, comprehension

R

RL.5.10

Informational Text

CCR

Read closely to determine what the text says explicitly and to make logical inferences from it; cite specific textual evidence when writing or speaking to support conclusions drawn from the text.

Standard

Quote accurately from a text when explaining what the text says explicitly and when drawing inferences from the text.

Enduring Understanding

Effective readers use a variety of strategies to make sense of key ideas and details presented in text.

Essential Questions

What do good readers do?
Am I clear about what I just read?
How do I know?

Suggested Learning Targets

I can quote ("word for word" support) accurately from a text. (S)
I can define inference and explain how a reader uses direct quotes from a text to reach a logical conclusion ("based on what I've read, it's most likely true that…"). (R)
I can read closely and find answers explicitly in text (right there answers) and answers that require an inference. (S)
I can analyze an author's words and find quotes needed to support both explicit and inferential questions. (S)

Vocabulary

quote, inference, explicit

R

RI.5.1

Informational Text

Key Ideas and Details

CCR

Determine central ideas or themes of a text and analyze their development; summarize the key supporting details and ideas.

Standard

Determine two or more main ideas of a text and explain how they are supported by key details; summarize the text.

Enduring Understanding

Effective readers use a variety of strategies to make sense of key ideas and details presented in text.

Essential Questions

What do good readers do?
Am I clear about what I just read?
How do I know?

Suggested Learning Targets

I can define main idea (who or what a text is mainly about). (K)
I can determine two or more main ideas of a text. (R)
I can identify key details in a text and explain how they support the main ideas. (R)
I can define summary (a shortened version of a text that states the key points). (K)
I can write a summary stating the key points of a text. (P)

Vocabulary

main idea, key detail, summary

R

RI.5.2

Informational Text

CCR

Analyze how and why individuals, events, and ideas develop and interact over the course of a text.

Standard

Explain the relationships or interactions between two or more individuals, events, ideas, or concepts in a historical, scientific, or technical text based on specific information in the text.

Enduring Understanding

Effective readers use a variety of strategies to make sense of key ideas and details presented in text.

Essential Questions

What do good readers do?
Am I clear about what I just read?
How do I know?

Suggested Learning Targets

I can identify individuals, events, ideas, and/or concepts in different types of text. (K)
I can use specific information in a text (e.g., historical, scientific, technical) to identify and explain the relationships between two or more individuals, events, ideas, and/or concepts. (R)
I can use specific information in a text (e.g., historical, scientific, technical) to identify and explain the interactions between two or more individuals, events, ideas, and/ or concepts. (R)

Vocabulary

relationship, interaction, individual, event, idea, concept

R   RI.5.3

Informational Text

CCR

Interpret words and phrases as they are used in a text, including determining technical, connotative, and figurative meanings, and analyze how specific word choices shape meaning or tone.

Standard

Determine the meaning of general academic and domain-specific words and phrases in a text relevant to a *grade 5 topic or subject area*.

Enduring Understanding

Analyzing texts for structure, purpose, and viewpoint allows an effective reader to gain insight and strengthen understanding.

Essential Questions

Author's choice: Why does it matter? What makes a story a "great" story?

Suggested Learning Targets

I can identify general academic words or phrases (different ways to say the same thing, e.g., *saunter* instead of *walk*) in a text. (K)

I can identify domain specific words or phrases (content words, e.g., *lava, democracy, pulley*) in a text. (K)

I can use various strategies (e.g., context clues, root words, affixes) to determine the meaning of general academic and domain-specific words and phrases in a text. (S)

I can locate and use resources (e.g., glossary, footnote, dictionary) to assist me in determining the meaning of unknown words and phrases. (S)

Vocabulary

general academic words, domain-specific words

R

RI.5.4

Informational Text

| Craft and Structure

CCR

Analyze the structure of texts, including how specific sentences, paragraphs, and larger portions of the text (e.g., a section, chapter, scene, or stanza) relate to each other and the whole.

Standard

Compare and contrast the overall structure (e.g., chronology, comparison, cause/effect, problem/solution) of events, ideas, concepts, or information in two or more texts.

Enduring Understanding

Analyzing texts for structure, purpose, and viewpoint allows an effective reader to gain insight and strengthen understanding.

Essential Questions

Author's choice: Why does it matter?
What makes a story a "great" story?

Suggested Learning Targets

I can identify and explain different structures used in informational text (e.g., chronology, compare/contrast, cause/effect, problem/solution). (K)
I can determine the overall structure of an informational text. (R)
I can compare (determine similarities) events, ideas, concepts, and/or information in two or more texts. (R)
I can contrast (determine differences) events, ideas, concepts, and/or information in two or more texts. (R)
I can analyze informational texts and determine if the structure chosen effectively relates events, ideas, concepts, or information. (R)

Vocabulary

text structure, compare, contrast

R

RI.5.5

Informational Text

Craft and Structure

CCR

Assess how point of view or purpose shapes the content and style of a text.

Standard

Analyze multiple accounts of the same event or topic, noting important similarities and differences in the point of view they represent.

Enduring Understanding

Analyzing texts for structure, purpose, and viewpoint allows an effective reader to gain insight and strengthen understanding.

Essential Questions

Author's choice: Why does it matter? What makes a story a "great" story?

Suggested Learning Targets

I can define point of view as how the author feels about the situation/topic of a text. (K)

I can determine an author's point of view (What do I know about the author's opinions, values, and/or beliefs?) and explain his/her purpose for writing the text. (R)

I can analyze how various authors develop the same event or topic and determine how each author's point of view affects the text. (R)

Vocabulary

point of view, purpose

R

RI.5.6

Informational Text

CCR

Integrate and evaluate content presented in diverse media and formats, including visually and quantitatively, as well as in words.*

Standard

Draw on information from multiple print or digital sources, demonstrating the ability to locate an answer to a question quickly or to solve a problem efficiently.

*Please see "Research to Build and Present Knowledge" in Writing and "Comprehension and Collaboration" in Speaking and Listening for additional standards relevant to gathering, assessing, and applying information from print and digital sources.

Enduring Understanding

To gain keener insight into the integration of knowledge and ideas, effective readers analyze and evaluate content, reasoning, and claims in diverse formats.

Essential Questions

In what ways does creative choice impact an audience?
Whose story is it, and why does it matter?

Suggested Learning Targets

I can recognize that authors use various formats when presenting information. (K)
I can identify information presented in formats (e.g., graphs, pictures, diagrams, charts, media clips) other than words. (K)
I can locate information from multiple print or digital sources to answer questions and solve problems quickly and efficiently. (S)

Vocabulary

format, print source, digital source, efficient

R

RI.5.7

Informational Text

CCR

Delineate and evaluate the argument and specific claims in a text, including the validity of the reasoning as well as the relevance and sufficiency of the evidence.

Standard

Explain how an author uses reasons and evidence to support particular points in a text, identifying which reasons and evidence support which point(s).

Enduring Understanding

To gain keener insight into the integration of knowledge and ideas, effective readers analyze and evaluate content, reasoning, and claims in diverse formats.

Essential Questions

In what ways does creative choice impact an audience?
Whose story is it, and why does it matter?

Suggested Learning Targets

I can locate the reasons and evidence an author uses to support particular points in a text. (K)
I can identify which reasons and evidence support particular points. (K)
I can explain how the reasons and evidence support the particular points in a text. (R)

Vocabulary

reasons, evidence

R

RI.5.8

Informational Text

CCR

Analyze how two or more texts address similar themes or topics in order to build knowledge or to compare the approaches the authors take.

Standard

Integrate information from several texts on the same topic in order to write or speak about the subject knowledgeably.

Enduring Understanding

To gain keener insight into the integration of knowledge and ideas, effective readers analyze and evaluate content, reasoning, and claims in diverse formats.

Essential Questions

In what ways does creative choice impact an audience?
Whose story is it, and why does it matter?

Suggested Learning Targets

I can locate information from several texts on the same topic. (S)
I can determine which pieces of information best support my topic. (R)
I can integrate (bring together) information from several texts to display my knowledge of the topic when writing or speaking. (S)

Vocabulary

integrate

R

RI.5.9

Informational Text

CCR

Read and comprehend complex literary and informational texts independently and proficiently.

Standard

By the end of the year, read and comprehend informational texts, including history/social studies, science, and technical texts, at the high end of the grades 4–5 text complexity band independently and proficiently.

Enduring Understanding

Students who are college and career ready read and interpret a variety of complex texts with confidence and independence.

Essential Questions

What do good readers do?
Am I clear about what I just read?
How do I know?

Suggested Learning Targets

I can closely read complex grade level texts. (S)
I can reread a text to find more information or clarify ideas. (S)
I can use reading strategies (e.g., ask questions, make connections, take notes, make inferences, visualize, re-read) to help me understand difficult complex text. (S)

Vocabulary

reading strategy, comprehension

R

RI.5.10

Foundational Skills

CCR

(Not applicable to Foundational Skills)

Standard

Know and apply grade-level phonics and word analysis skills in decoding words.

a. Use combined knowledge of all letter-sound correspondences, syllabication patterns, and morphology (e.g., roots and affixes) to read accurately unfamiliar multisyllabic words in context and out of context.

*Standards 1 and 2 are taught in grades K-1.

Enduring Understanding

Word analysis and decoding skills are foundational for success as a reader.

Essential Questions

How do sounds and letters create words?

When a word doesn't make sense, what can I do?

Suggested Learning Targets

I can recognize that letters and combinations of letters (graphemes) make different sounds (phonemes). (K)

I can use my knowledge of consonant blends, long-vowel patterns and short-vowel patterns to decode words. (S)

I can analyze the structure of words by finding compound words, roots, prefixes, suffixes, and syllables. (R)

I can use my analysis of word structure to help me decode unfamiliar multi-syllabic words. (S)

Vocabulary

consonant blend, long-vowel pattern, short-vowel pattern, root, prefix, suffix, syllable

R   RF.5.3

Foundational Skills

CCR

(Not applicable to Foundational Skills)

Standard

Read with sufficient accuracy and fluency to support comprehension.
a. Read grade-level text with purpose and understanding.
b. Read grade-level prose and poetry orally with accuracy, appropriate rate, and expression.
c. Use context to confirm or self-correct word recognition and understanding, rereading as necessary.

Enduring Understanding

Fluent readers accurately process print with expression at an appropriate rate.

Essential Questions

What do good readers do?
Why does fluency matter?

Suggested Learning Targets

I can read grade-level text fluently and show comprehension through voice, timing, and expression. (S)
I can recognize when a word I have read does not make sense within the text. (K)
I can self-correct misread or misunderstood words using context clues. (S)
I can reread with corrections when necessary. (S)
I can read fluently (easy, smooth, and automatic). (S)

Vocabulary

fluency, context clue

R

RF.5.4

Writing

CCR

Write arguments to support claims in an analysis of substantive topics or texts, using valid reasoning and relevant and sufficient evidence.

Standard

Write opinion pieces on topics or texts, supporting a point of view with reasons and information.

a. Introduce a topic or text clearly, state an opinion, and create an organizational structure in which ideas are logically grouped to support the writer's purpose.
b. Provide logically ordered reasons that are supported by facts and details.
c. Link opinion and reasons using words, phrases, and clauses (e.g., *consequently*, *specifically*).
d. Provide a concluding statement or section related to the opinion presented.

*These broad types of writing include many subgenres. See Appendix A for definitions of key writing types.

Enduring Understanding

Writing should be purposely focused, detailed, organized, and sequenced in a way that clearly communicates the ideas to the reader.

Essential Questions

What do good writers do?
What's my purpose and how do I develop it?

Suggested Learning Targets

I can determine my opinion/point of view on a particular topic or text. (R)
I can create an organizational structure (chronology, compare/contrast, cause/effect, problem/solution) to logically introduce my topic and opinion. (S)
I can support my opinion with logically ordered facts and details and link my reasons with words, phrases, and clauses. (S)
I can write an opinion piece with an introduction, supporting details/facts, and a concluding statement/section. (P)

Vocabulary

opinion, point of view, organizational structure

W   W.5.1

Writing

CCR

Write informative/explanatory texts to examine and convey complex ideas and information clearly and accurately through the effective selection, organization, and analysis of content.

Standard

Write informative/explanatory texts to examine a topic and convey ideas and information clearly.

a. Introduce a topic clearly, provide a general observation and focus, and group related information logically; include formatting (e.g., headings), illustrations, and multimedia when useful to aiding comprehension.

b. Develop the topic with facts, definitions, concrete details, quotations, or other information and examples related to the topic.

c. Link ideas within and across categories of information using words, phrases, and clauses (e.g., *in contrast, especially*).

d. Use precise language and domain-specific vocabulary to inform about or explain the topic.

e. Provide a concluding statement or section related to the information or explanation presented.

*These broad types of writing include many subgenres. See Appendix A for definitions of key writing types.

Enduring Understanding

Writing should be purposely focused, detailed, organized, and sequenced in a way that clearly communicates the ideas to the reader.

Essential Questions

What do good writers do?
What's my purpose and how do I develop it?

Suggested Learning Targets

I can select a topic and gather information (e.g., facts, definitions, concrete details, quotations, examples) to share with my audience. (S)

I can define common formatting structures and determine structures that will allow me to organize my information best. (R)

(continued on next page)

Vocabulary

formatting structure, observation, focus, multimedia, precise, domain-specific vocabulary

W

W.5.2

Writing

CCR

Write informative/explanatory texts to examine and convey complex ideas and information clearly and accurately through the effective selection, organization, and analysis of content.

Standard

Write informative/explanatory texts to examine a topic and convey ideas and information clearly.

a. Introduce a topic clearly, provide a general observation and focus, and group related information logically; include formatting (e.g., headings), illustrations, and multimedia when useful to aiding comprehension.
b. Develop the topic with facts, definitions, concrete details, quotations, or other information and examples related to the topic.
c. Link ideas within and across categories of information using words, phrases, and clauses (e.g., in contrast, especially).
d. Use precise language and domain-specific vocabulary to inform about or explain the topic.
e. Provide a concluding statement or section related to the information or explanation presented.

These broad types of writing include many subgenres. See Appendix A for definitions of key writing types.

Suggested Learning Targets

(continued from previous page)

I can introduce my topic by providing my general observation/focus and use formatting structures, illustrations, and multimedia to clarify (make clear) my topic. (S)

I can link my information (e.g., facts, definitions, details, quotations, examples) using words, phrases, and clauses. (S)

I can explain my topic using precise language and domain-specific vocabulary. (S)

I can present my information in a formal style with a concluding statement or section that relates to the information presented. (P)

Writing

CCR

Write narratives to develop real or imagined experiences or events using effective technique, well-chosen details, and well-structured event sequences.

Standard

Write narratives to develop real or imagined experiences or events using effective technique, descriptive details, and clear event sequences.

a.   Orient the reader by establishing a situation and introducing a narrator and/or characters; organize an event sequence that unfolds naturally.

b.   Use narrative techniques, such as dialogue, description, and pacing, to develop experiences and events or show the responses of characters to situations.

c.   Use a variety of transitional words, phrases, and clauses to manage the sequence of events.

d.   Use concrete words and phrases and sensory details to convey experiences and events precisely.

e.   Provide a conclusion that follows from the narrated experiences or events.

*These broad types of writing include many subgenres. See Appendix A for definitions of key writing types.

Enduring Understanding

Writing should be purposely focused, detailed, organized, and sequenced in a way that clearly communicates the ideas to the reader.

Essential Questions

What do good writers do?
What's my purpose and how do I develop it?

Suggested Learning Targets

I can define narrative and describe the basic parts of plot (exposition, rising action, climax, falling action, and resolution). (K)

I can orient (set the scene for) the reader by introducing the narrator, characters, and the event/situation that starts the story in motion. (S)

I can sequence the events in my story so that one event logically leads to the next. (R)

(continued on next page)

Vocabulary

narrative, narrator, sequence, concrete word, sensory detail, transition, conclusion

W

W.5.3

Writing

CCR

Write narratives to develop real or imagined experiences or events using effective technique, well-chosen details, and well-structured event sequences.

Standard

Write narratives to develop real or imagined experiences or events using effective technique, descriptive details, and clear event sequences.

a. Orient the reader by establishing a situation and introducing a narrator and/or characters; organize an event sequence that unfolds naturally.

b. Use narrative techniques, such as dialogue, description, and pacing, to develop experiences and events or show the responses of characters to situations.

c. Use a variety of transitional words, phrases, and clauses to manage the sequence of events.

d. Use concrete words and phrases and sensory details to convey experiences and events precisely.

e. Provide a conclusion that follows from the narrated experiences or events.

*These broad types of writing include many subgenres. See Appendix A for definitions of key writing types.

Suggested Learning Targets

(continued from previous page)

I can use narrative techniques (e.g., dialogue, description, pacing) to develop events and/or experiences and show how characters respond to situations. (S)

I can use concrete words and phrases as well as sensory details (descriptive words and phrases that appeal to the senses) to help my reader understand the experiences and events (create mind pictures). (S)

I can signal changes in time and place by using transition words, phrases, and clauses. (S)

I can write a logical conclusion that provides a sense of closure (ties up all the loose ends and leaves the reader satisfied). (P)

Writing

CCR

Produce clear and coherent writing in which the development, organization, and style are appropriate to task, purpose, and audience.

Standard

Produce clear and coherent writing in which the development and organization are appropriate to task, purpose, and audience. (Grade-specific expectations for writing types are defined in standards 1–3 above.)

Enduring Understanding

Producing clear ideas as a writer involves selecting appropriate style and structure for an audience and is strengthened through revision and technology.

Essential Questions

Writing clearly: What makes a difference?
Final product: What does it take?

Suggested Learning Targets

I can identify the writing style (e.g., argument, informative/explanatory, narrative) that best fits my task, purpose, and audience. (K)
I can use organizational/formatting structures (graphic organizers) to develop my writing ideas. (S)
I can compose a clear and logical piece of writing that demonstrates my understanding of a specific writing style. (P)

Vocabulary

writing style, task, purpose, audience

W

W.5.4

Writing

CCR

Develop and strengthen writing as needed by planning, revising, editing, rewriting, or trying a new approach.

Standard

With guidance and support from peers and adults, develop and strengthen writing as needed by planning, revising, editing, rewriting, or trying a new approach. (Editing for conventions should demonstrate command of Language standards 1–3 up to and including grade 5.)

Enduring Understanding

Producing clear ideas as a writer involves selecting appropriate style and structure for an audience and is strengthened through revision and technology.

Essential Questions

Writing clearly: What makes a difference?
Final product: What does it take?

Suggested Learning Targets

I can use prewriting strategies to formulate ideas (e.g., graphic organizers, brainstorming, lists). (S)
I can recognize that a well-developed piece of writing requires more than one draft. (K)
I can apply revision strategies (reading aloud, checking for misunderstandings, adding and deleting details) with the help of others. (S)
I can edit my writing by checking for errors in capitalization, punctuation, grammar, spelling, etc. (S)
I can prepare multiple drafts using revisions and edits to develop and strengthen my writing. (S)
I can recognize when revising, editing, and rewriting are not enough, and I need to try a new approach. (K)

Vocabulary

revision strategy, edit

W

W.5.5

Writing

Production and Distribution of Writing

CCR

Use technology, including the Internet, to produce and publish writing and to interact and collaborate with others.

Standard

With some guidance and support from adults, use technology, including the Internet, to produce and publish writing as well as to interact and collaborate with others; demonstrate sufficient command of keyboarding skills to type a minimum of two pages in a single sitting.

Enduring Understanding

Producing clear ideas as a writer involves selecting appropriate style and structure for an audience and is strengthened through revision and technology.

Essential Questions

Writing clearly: What makes a difference?
Final product: What does it take?

Suggested Learning Targets

I can identify technology (e.g., Word, Publisher, PowerPoint) that will help me produce, edit, and publish my writing. (K)
I can choose credible websites on the Internet that will help me compose, edit, and publish my writing. (S)
I can collaborate with peers, teachers, and others to produce and publish my writing. (S)
I can use proper keyboarding skills (type a minimum of two pages in a single sitting) to compose and prepare my writing for publication. (S)

Vocabulary

publish, credible website

W

W.5.6

Writing

CCR

Conduct short as well as more sustained research projects based on focused questions, demonstrating understanding of the subject under investigation.

Standard

Conduct short research projects that use several sources to build knowledge through investigation of different aspects of a topic.

Enduring Understanding

Effective research presents an answer to a question, demonstrates understanding of the inquiry, and properly cites information from multiple sources.

Essential Questions

What do good researchers do?
"Cut and Paste:" What's the problem?

Suggested Learning Targets

I can define research and explain how research is different from other types of writing. (R)

I can focus my research around a central question that is provided or determine my own research worthy question (e.g., *Why do birds migrate?*). (S)

I can choose several sources (e.g., biographies, non-fiction texts, online encyclopedia) and gather information to answer my research question. (S)

I can analyze the information found in my sources and determine if it provides enough support to answer my question. (R)

Vocabulary

research, central question, source

W

W.5.7

Writing

CCR

Gather relevant information from multiple print and digital sources, assess the credibility and accuracy of each source, and integrate the information while avoiding plagiarism.

Standard

Recall relevant information from experiences or gather relevant information from print and digital sources; summarize or paraphrase information in notes and finished work, and provide a list of sources.

Enduring Understanding

Effective research presents an answer to a question, demonstrates understanding of the inquiry, and properly cites information from multiple sources.

Essential Questions

What do good researchers do?
"Cut and Paste:" What's the problem?

Suggested Learning Targets

I can recall information from experiences or gather information from print and digital sources about a topic. (S)
I can summarize and/or paraphrase (put in my own words) information when taking notes and preparing my finished work. (R)
I can prepare a list of sources used in my research. (P)

Vocabulary

summarize, paraphrase, source

W

W.5.8

Writing

CCR

Draw evidence from literary or informational texts to support analysis, reflection, and research.

Standard

Draw evidence from literary or informational texts to support analysis, reflection, and research.

a. Apply *grade 5 Reading standards* to literature (e.g., "Compare and contrast two or more characters, settings, or events in a story or a drama, drawing on specific details in the text [e.g., how characters interact]").

b. Apply *grade 5 Reading standards* to informational texts (e.g., "Explain how an author uses reasons and evidence to support particular points in a text, identifying which reasons and evidence support which point[s]").

Enduring Understanding

Effective research presents an answer to a question, demonstrates understanding of the inquiry, and properly cites information from multiple sources.

Essential Questions

What do good researchers do?
"Cut and Paste:" What's the problem?

Suggested Learning Targets

I can define textual evidence ("word for word" support). (K)
I can determine textual evidence that supports my analysis, reflection, and/or research. (R)
I can compose written responses and include textual evidence to strengthen my analysis, reflection, and/or research. (P)

Vocabulary

analysis, reflection, research

W

W.5.9

Writing

CCR

Write routinely over extended time frames (time for research, reflection, and revision) and shorter time frames (a single sitting or a day or two) for a range of tasks, purposes, and audiences.

Standard

Write routinely over extended time frames (time for research, reflection, and revision) and shorter time frames (a single sitting or a day or two) for a range of discipline-specific tasks, purposes, and audiences.

Enduring Understanding

Effective writers use a variety of formats to communicate ideas appropriate for the audience, task, and time frame.

Essential Questions

Why write?
What do good writers do?

Suggested Learning Targets

I can recognize that different writing tasks (e.g., journal, reflection, research) require varied time frames to complete. (K)

I can determine a writing format/style to fit my task, purpose, and/or audience. (R)

I can write for a variety of reasons (e.g., to inform, to describe, to persuade, to entertain/convey an experience). (P)

Vocabulary

writing format, writing style, task, purpose, audience

W

W.5.10

Speaking and Listening

CCR

Prepare for and participate effectively in a range of conversations and collaborations with diverse partners, building on others' ideas and expressing their own clearly and persuasively.

Standard

Engage effectively in a range of collaborative discussions (one-on-one, in groups, and teacher-led) with diverse partners on *grade 5 topics and texts*, building on others' ideas and expressing their own clearly.

a. Come to discussions prepared, having read or studied required material; explicitly draw on that preparation and other information known about the topic to explore ideas under discussion.
b. Follow agreed-upon rules for discussions and carry out assigned roles.
c. Pose and respond to specific questions by making comments that contribute to the discussion and elaborate on the remarks of others.
d. Review the key ideas expressed and draw conclusions in light of information and knowledge gained from the discussions.

Enduring Understanding

Comprehension is enhanced through a collaborative process of sharing and evaluating ideas.

Essential Questions

What makes collaboration meaningful?
Making meaning from a variety of sources: What will help?

Suggested Learning Targets

I can read or study material(s) to be discussed. (S)
I can list important information about the topic to be discussed. (K)
I can identify and follow the agreed upon rules for discussion and carry out assigned roles. (P)
I can ask questions when I do not understand. (S)
I can stay on topic by making comments about the information being discussed. (S)
I can make connections between the comments of others. (S).
I can explain my own ideas and tell what I've learned from a discussion. (S)

Vocabulary

discussion, connection

SL

SL.5.1

Speaking and Listening

CCR

Integrate and evaluate information presented in diverse media and formats, including visually, quantitatively, and orally.

Standard

Summarize a written text read aloud or information presented in diverse media and formats, including visually, quantitatively, and orally.

Enduring Understanding

Comprehension is enhanced through a collaborative process of sharing and evaluating ideas.

Essential Questions

What makes collaboration meaningful? Making meaning from a variety of sources: What will help?

Suggested Learning Targets

I can identify information from a text being read aloud. (K)
I can identify information that is presented in different formats (e.g., media, charts, graphs, websites, speeches). (K)
I can summarize the information gathered to determine the main idea and support details of a presentation. (S)

Vocabulary

format, main idea, supporting details

SL

SL.5.2

Speaking and Listening

CCR

Evaluate a speaker's point of view, reasoning, and use of evidence and rhetoric.

Standard

Summarize the points a speaker makes and explain how each claim is supported by reasons and evidence.

Enduring Understanding

Comprehension is enhanced through a collaborative process of sharing and evaluating ideas.

Essential Questions

What makes collaboration meaningful?
Making meaning from a variety of sources: What will help?

Suggested Learning Targets

I can identify a speaker's claims that are supported by reasons and evidence. (K)
I can summarize a speaker's points using reasons and evidence he/she provides to support his/her claims. (S)

Vocabulary

claim, reason, evidence, summary

SL

SL.5.3

Speaking and Listening

Presentation of Knowledge and Ideas

CCR

Present information, findings, and supporting evidence such that listeners can follow the line of reasoning and the organization, development, and style are appropriate to task, purpose, and audience.

Standard

Report on a topic or text or present an opinion, sequencing ideas logically and using appropriate facts and relevant, descriptive details to support main ideas or themes; speak clearly at an understandable pace.

Enduring Understanding

Presentation of knowledge and ideas is enhanced through appropriate organization and style for an audience via the use of visual displays, technology, and the appropriate use of language.

Essential Questions

What makes a presentation "great"?
"What I say" versus "how I say it", does it really matter?

Suggested Learning Targets

I can determine a logical sequence for presenting my ideas and facts. (R)
I can present my ideas and/or opinion with facts and relevant (appropriate) descriptive details that support the main idea or theme. (S)
I can report my information by speaking clearly at an appropriate pace. (S)

Vocabulary

logical sequence, relevant, main idea, theme, pace

SL

SL.5.4

Speaking and Listening

CCR

Make strategic use of digital media and visual displays of data to express information and enhance understanding of presentations.

Standard

Include multimedia components (e.g., graphics, sound) and visual displays in presentations when appropriate to enhance the development of main ideas or themes.

Enduring Understanding

Presentation of knowledge and ideas is enhanced through appropriate organization and style for an audience via the use of visual displays, technology, and the appropriate use of language.

Essential Questions

What makes a presentation "great"?
"What I say" versus "how I say it", does it really matter?

Suggested Learning Targets

I can identify main ideas or themes in my presentation that could be enhanced. (K)
I can determine and include an appropriate multimedia component or visual display to enhance my main ideas or themes. (S)

Vocabulary

main idea, theme, enhance, multimedia component, visual display

SL   SL.5.5

Speaking and Listening

CCR

Adapt speech to a variety of contexts and communicative tasks, demonstrating command of formal English when indicated or appropriate.

Standard

Adapt speech to a variety of contexts and tasks, using formal English when appropriate to task and situation. (See grade 5 Language standards 1 and 3 for specific expectations.)

Enduring Understanding

Presentation of knowledge and ideas is enhanced through appropriate organization and style for an audience via the use of visual displays, technology, and the appropriate use of language.

Essential Questions

What makes a presentation "great"?
"What I say" versus "how I say it", does it really matter?

Suggested Learning Targets

I can identify various reasons for speaking (e.g., informational, descriptive, formal, informal). (K)
I can adapt a speech for various tasks or situations. (S)
I can compose a formal speech that demonstrates a command of grade 5 Language standards. (P)

Vocabulary

formal, informal

SL

SL.5.6

Language

CCR

Demonstrate command of the conventions of standard English grammar and usage when writing or speaking.

Standard

Demonstrate command of the conventions of standard English grammar and usage when writing or speaking.

a. Explain the function of conjunctions, prepositions, and interjections in general and their function in particular sentences.
b. Form and use the perfect (e.g., *I had walked; I have walked; I will have walked*) verb tenses.
c. Use verb tense to convey various times, sequences, states, and conditions.
d. Recognize and correct inappropriate shifts in verb tense.*
e. Use correlative conjunctions (e.g., *either/or, neither/nor*).

* See ELA CCSS Appendix A, page 31 for Language Progressive Skills.

Enduring Understanding

Effective communication of ideas when speaking or writing relies on the appropriate use of the conventions of language.

Essential Questions

Why do the rules of language matter?
Communicating clearly: What does it take?

Suggested Learning Targets

I can define conjunction (word(s) that connect words, phrases, clauses, or sentences) and explain its function in a sentence. (R)
I can define preposition (a word that shows a relationship of a noun or pronoun to another word in a sentence) and explain its function in a sentence. (R)

(continued on next page)

Vocabulary

conjunction, preposition, interjection, past perfect, present perfect, future perfect, verb tense, correlative conjunction

L

L.5.1

Language

CCR

Demonstrate command of the conventions of standard English grammar and usage when writing or speaking.

Standard

Demonstrate command of the conventions of standard English grammar and usage when writing or speaking.

- a. Explain the function of conjunctions, prepositions, and interjections in general and their function in particular sentences.
- b. Form and use the perfect (e.g., *I had walked; I have walked; I will have walked*) verb tenses.
- c. Use verb tense to convey various times, sequences, states, and conditions.
- d. Recognize and correct inappropriate shifts in verb tense.*
- e. Use correlative conjunctions (e.g., *either/or, neither/nor*).

* See ELA CCSS Appendix A, page 31 for Language Progressive Skills.

Suggested Learning Targets

(continued from previous page)

I can define interjection (an exclamation or attention getter that expresses strong feeling and usually comes at the beginning of a sentence) and explain its function in a sentence. (R)

I can identify the past perfect, present perfect, and future perfect verb tenses and use them correctly. (S)

I can choose the correct verb tense to show time, sequence, state, and condition. (S)

I can identify when the incorrect verb tense has been used and make appropriate corrections. (S)

I can identify common correlative conjunctions and use them correctly when writing. (S)

L

L.5.1 *(cont.)*

Language

CCR

Demonstrate command of the conventions of standard English capitalization, punctuation, and spelling when writing.

Standard

Demonstrate command of the conventions of standard English capitalization, punctuation, and spelling when writing.

a. Use punctuation to separate items in a series.*
b. Use a comma to separate an introductory element from the rest of the sentence.
c. Use a comma to set off the words *yes* and *no* (e.g., *Yes, thank you*), to set off a tag question from the rest of the sentence (e.g., *It's true, isn't it?*), and to indicate direct address (e.g., *Is that you, Steve?*).
d. Use underlining, quotation marks, or italics to indicate titles of works.
e. Spell grade-appropriate words correctly, consulting references as needed.

* See ELA CCSS Appendix A, page 31 for Language Progressive Skills.

Enduring Understanding

Effective communication of ideas when speaking or writing relies on the appropriate use of the conventions of language.

Essential Questions

Why do the rules of language matter?
Communicating clearly: What does it take?

Suggested Learning Targets

I can determine when to capitalize words (e.g., proper nouns, "I", first word in a sentence). (R)
I can identify items in a series and punctuate them correctly. (S)
I can identify an introductory element (e.g., interjection, prepositional phrase of three or more words, adverb clause) and use a comma to separate it from the rest of a sentence. (S)
I can identify when a comma should be used to set off the words yes and no, tag questions, and direct address. (S)
I can identify titles of works and choose the correct formatting style (e.g., underlining, quotation marks, italics). (S)
I can identify misspelled words and use resources to assist me in spelling correctly. (S)

Vocabulary

items in a series, introductory element, tag questions, direct address

L   L.5.2

Language

Knowledge of Language

CCR

Apply knowledge of language to understand how language functions in different contexts, to make effective choices for meaning or style, and to comprehend more fully when reading or listening.

Standard

Use knowledge of language and its conventions when writing, speaking, reading, or listening.

a. Expand, combine, and reduce sentences for meaning, reader/listener interest, and style.
b. Compare and contrast the varieties of English (e.g., dialects, registers) used in stories, dramas, or poems.

Enduring Understanding

Effective readers, writers, and listeners use knowledge of language to make appropriate choices when presenting information and to clarify meaning when reading or listening.

Essential Questions

How does situation affect meaning?
How does author's choice impact an audience?

Suggested Learning Targets

I can identify simple sentence structures (one independent clause), compound sentence structures (two or more independent clauses), and complex sentence structures (one independent clause and one or more subordinate clauses) sentence structures. (K)
I can determine when to use varied sentence structures to create meaning, interest, and style in my writing. (R)
I can compare (determine similarities) how authors use variations of English in stories, dramas, or poems (e.g., dialect – *Two authors use "ya'll" when writing dialogue for characters in the South.*). (R)
I can contrast (determine differences) how authors use variations of English in stories, dramas, or poems (e.g., formal register – *"I would be so grateful if you would stop talking." versus informal register – "Shut your mouth."*). (R)

Vocabulary

simple sentence structure, compound sentence structure, complex sentence structure, style, compare, contrast, register, dialect

L

L.5.3

Language

CCR

Determine or clarify the meaning of unknown and multiple-meaning words and phrases by using context clues, analyzing meaningful word parts, and consulting general and specialized reference materials, as appropriate.

Standard

Determine or clarify the meaning of unknown and multiple-meaning words and phrases based on *grade 5 reading and content*, choosing flexibly from a range of strategies.

   a. Use context (e.g., cause/effect relationships and comparisons in text) as a clue to the meaning of a word or phrase.

   b. Use common, grade-appropriate Greek and Latin affixes and roots as clues to the meaning of a word (e.g., *photograph, photosynthesis*).

   c. Consult reference materials (e.g., dictionaries, glossaries, thesauruses), both print and digital, to find the pronunciation and determine or clarify the precise meaning of key words and phrases.

Enduring Understanding

Effective readers and writers use knowledge of the structure and context of language to acquire, clarify, and appropriately use vocabulary.

Essential Questions

When a word doesn't make sense, what can I do?

How do I use what I know to figure out what I don't know?

Suggested Learning Targets

I can infer the meaning of unknown words using context clues (e.g., definitions, synonyms/antonyms, cause/effect relationships, comparisons found in surrounding text). (R)

I can recognize and define common Greek and Latin affixes and roots (units of meaning). (K)

I can break down unknown words into units of meaning to infer the definition. (R)

I can verify my inferred meaning of an unknown word by consulting reference materials (e.g., dictionaries, glossaries, thesauruses). (S)

Vocabulary

infer, context clue, affix, root

L

L.5.4

Language

CCR

Demonstrate understanding of word relationships and nuances in word meanings.

Standard

Demonstrate understanding of figurative language, word relationships, and nuances in word meanings.

   a.   Interpret figurative language, including similes and metaphors, in context.
   b.   Recognize and explain the meaning of common idioms, adages, and proverbs.
   c.   Use the relationship between particular words (e.g., synonyms, antonyms, homographs) to better understand each of the words.

Enduring Understanding

Effective readers and writers use knowledge of the structure and context of language to acquire, clarify, and appropriately use vocabulary.

Essential Questions

When a word doesn't make sense, what can I do?

How do I use what I know to figure out what I don't know?

Suggested Learning Targets

I can define and identify various forms of figurative language (e.g., simile, metaphor, hyperbole, personification, alliteration, onomatopoeia). (K)

I can distinguish between literal language (it means exactly what it says) and figurative language (sometimes what you say is not exactly what you mean). (R)

I can recognize when an author is using idioms, adages, and proverbs and determine his/her intended meaning. (R)

I can recognize word relationships and use the relationships to further understand each of the words (e.g., *pretty/gorgeous, love/loathe, Because there was no wind, I had to wind up my kite string and go home.*). (S)

Vocabulary

figurative language, literal language, idiom, adage, proverb, word relationships

L

L.5.5

Language

CCR

Acquire and use accurately a range of general academic and domain-specific words and phrases sufficient for reading, writing, speaking, and listening at the college and career readiness level; demonstrate independence in gathering vocabulary knowledge when encountering an unknown term important to comprehension or expression.

Standard

Acquire and use accurately grade-appropriate general academic and domain-specific words and phrases, including those that signal contrast, addition, and other logical relationships (e.g., *however, although, nevertheless, similarly, moreover, in addition*).

Enduring Understanding

Effective readers and writers use knowledge of the structure and context of language to acquire, clarify, and appropriately use vocabulary.

Essential Questions

When a word doesn't make sense, what can I do?
How do I use what I know to figure out what I don't know?

Suggested Learning Targets

I can recognize the difference between general academic words and phrases (Tier Two words are subtle or precise ways to say relatively precise things, e.g., *saunter* instead of *walk*.) and domain-specific words and phrases (Tier Three words are often specific to content knowledge, e.g., *lava, democracy, pulley*.).* (K)

I can acquire and use grade-appropriate academic and domain-specific words/phrases, including words that signal contrast, addition, and other logical relationships, to increase comprehension and expression. (S)

*Tier One, Tier Two, and Tier Three words are clarified on pages 33-35 of Appendix A in the Common Core Standards.

Vocabulary

general academic words, domain-specific word

L   **L.5.6**